D1314424

WITHDRAWN

The First Men on the Moon

History Maker Bios

Stephanie Sammartino McPherson

LERNER PUBLICATIONS COMPANY • MINNEAPOLIS

For my husband Dick and my daughters, Jennifer and Marianne

Special thanks to my editor, Mary Winget, for her perceptive comments and to Dick McPherson and Marion and Angelo Sammartino for their encouragement

Illustrations by Bill Hauser

Text copyright © 2009 by Stephanie Sammartino McPherson
Illustrations copyright © 2009 by Lerner Publishing Group, Inc.

Lerner Publications Company
A division of Lerner Publishing Group, Inc.
241 First Avenue North
Minneapolis, MN 55401 U.S.A.

Website address: www.lernerbooks.com

Library of Congress Cataloging-in-Publication Data

McPherson, Stephanie Sammartino.
    The first men on the moon / by Stephanie Sammartino McPherson.
        p. cm. — (History maker biographies)
    Includes bibliographical references and index.
    ISBN 978–0–7613–4949–5 (lb. bdg. : alk. paper)
        1. Astronauts—United States—Biography—Juvenile literature. 2. Project Apollo (U.S.)—Juvenile literature. I. Title. II. Title: Apollo Eleven astronauts.
    TL789.85.A1M325 2009
    629.450092'273—dc22 [B]   2009001864

Manufactured in the United States of America
1 2 3 4 5 6 – PA – 14 13 12 11 10 09

TABLE OF CONTENTS

INTRODUCTION

Some people thought the day would never come. For centuries, the moon had fascinated everyone on Earth. But the moon is about 240,000 miles away. Visiting the moon seemed an impossible dream. Finally, the dream was about to come true.

In every country, people sat spellbound before their television sets. A tiny spacecraft called the *Eagle* had landed on the moon. Thousands of workers had made it possible. But on July 20, 1969, everyone was focused on Neil Armstrong, Buzz Aldrin, and Mike Collins. Neil and Buzz became the first men to walk on the moon. High above them, Mike Collins circled the moon in the mother ship, *Columbia*. The men's names would forever be linked to one of history's greatest moments.

This is their story.

1 LOVE OF FLYING

Air travel was an exciting experience in 1930. That was the year Neil Armstrong, Buzz Aldrin, and Michael Collins were born. Less than thirty years had passed since the brothers Wilbur and Orville Wright had made the first true airplane flight. Eagerly, the public followed each new development in flying. But few people had a chance to ride in an airplane.

Neil was young when he started to love airplanes.

To Neil Armstrong, however, airplanes were almost a way of life. He was the oldest of Stephen and Viola Armstrong's three children. Neil was born in Wapakoneta, Ohio. His father's job took the family all over the state. He worked for the state government.

When Neil was about six, his family lived in Warren. A pilot at the small Warren Airport offered rides to the public for twenty-five cents. Stephen decided this would be a fine adventure for his little boy.

Neil and his father flew in an airplane called a Tin Goose. It had three motors and could go 130 miles per hour. The plane shook. The engine roared. "I was scared to death," Neil's father later admitted. Not Neil. Neil had had fun.

Neil made this model of an airplane.

As he grew up, Neil couldn't get enough of airplanes. He liked to build model planes. He hung them from the ceiling of his bedroom. He also read everything he could find about flying. But books and models weren't enough. By the time Neil was fourteen, he wanted to learn to fly.

Flying lessons at the local airport cost nine dollars an hour. Neil had odd jobs at several stores. But he never made more than forty cents per hour. He had to work twenty-two and one-half hours to pay for one lesson. But to Neil it was worth the effort. On his sixteenth birthday, he earned his pilot's license. Nothing could have made him happier.

Buzz Aldrin also wanted to be a pilot at an early age. Like Neil, he grew up learning a lot about airplanes. His father, Gene Aldrin, had been a U.S. Army pilot during World War I (1914–1918). Flying was a popular subject in the Aldrin home.

Gene and his wife, Marion Moon Aldrin, had three children. Their only son was born on January 20, 1930. By that time, Gene had retired from the army. The family had settled in a large house in Montclair, New Jersey.

Gene and Marion named their youngest child Edwin. One of his sisters wanted to call him brother. But she was still so young that she could only say "buzzer." Later, the name got shortened to Buzz, and it stuck.

Buzz (LEFT) first learned about flying from his father (RIGHT).

Buzz took his first airplane ride when he was only two years old. Through the years, he flew with his father several times. And he spent hours working on model airplanes. He made them as perfect as he could.

Although he was small for his age, Buzz liked to wrestle and play football. He didn't worry much about his studies. But that changed around the time Buzz started high school. By then, he knew he wanted to be a pilot. Buzz began to study hard and make good grades. He would have to go to a good college if he wanted to fly airplanes someday.

Buzz played on his high school football team.

When Mike was young, he had a dog named Punch.

Michael Collins had something in common with Buzz. He also came from an army family. The youngest child of General and Mrs. James Collins, Mike was born in Rome, Italy. But the family didn't stay there long. The Collinses moved back to the United States. Growing up, Mike lived in Oklahoma, New York, Maryland, Ohio, and Texas. He enjoyed riding horses, hiking through the woods, and fishing near the Chesapeake Bay in Maryland.

Mike had his first airplane ride in Puerto Rico, an island south of the United States. To his delight, the pilot let him try his hand at steering. Up and down went the nose of the plane as Mike struggled with the controls.

A man reads a newspaper about the U.S. entering the war.

The United States entered World War II (1939–1945) in 1941. The Collins family then moved to Washington, D.C. Neil, Buzz, and Mike were too young to fight in the war. But they were old enough to follow news of the war. They knew that U.S. airpower would play a major role in beating the enemy. Bigger, faster planes were being built every month. This helped the science of aviation, or flying, to change fast too.

2 "SPACE IS THE FRONTIER"

World War II had ended in 1945. The nation was moving forward. And so were Neil, Buzz, and Mike. They were thinking about college. Buzz and Mike went to the U.S. Military Academy at West Point, New York. Neil got a scholarship from the U.S. Navy. The money helped him pay for going to Purdue University in Indiana.

All three young men served in the military. Neil's turn came first. A year and a half after he had entered college, the navy called him to active duty. The United States was fighting the Korean War (1950–1953). Neil trained as a fighter pilot. Then the navy sent him to Korea. There, he flew seventy-eight combat missions.

One time, Neil flew through an enemy cable that damaged his wing. He could not save his plane. Neil bailed out and landed in a rice paddy. To his great surprise, a friend from flight school came by in a jeep. Soon he was safely back with his unit.

Neil learned to fly fighter planes in the military. After the Korean War ended, Neil got a job studying fighter planes.

Buzz also fought in Korea. As a U.S. Air Force fighter pilot, he flew sixty-seven combat missions. Mike Collins had a different experience. He joined the air force too. But he was sent to California instead of Korea. Later, he received orders to France, where he continued to fly.

Mike joined the U.S. Air Force when he was in college. This is Mike in his last year of college.

The 1950s were an exciting time to be a pilot. New planes were being developed. They flew higher and faster than ever before. Neil and Mike wanted to be part of the great adventure. They wanted to test new aircraft before the planes were put into military service.

Being a test pilot was a serious job. Fighter pilots have only their own safety to think about. But test pilots have to think about the people who may fly the plane in the future. Test pilots have to be very careful in judging what a plane can safely do.

Some new planes like the Skyrockets (RIGHT) were known for their great speed.

John Glenn prepares for his mission.

The U.S. space program was moving ahead too. On February 20, 1962, John Glenn became the second person in the world and the first American to orbit, or circle, Earth. All over the country people celebrated. Space pilots, called astronauts, were big news.

No one was more excited than Mike Collins. He enjoyed testing new planes at Edwards Air Force Base in California. But no plane could do what John Glenn had done. How amazing to circle the whole world in ninety minutes! Mike began to think about becoming an astronaut.

Neil tested new planes like this X-15.

Neil Armstrong was also at Edwards Air Force Base. Like Mike, he loved testing planes. In April 1962, he took the most advanced plane of all, the X-15, to 200,000 feet above Earth. At that height, he could see the curve of Earth's surface. Neil's experience thrilled him so much that he wanted to go higher. "Space is the frontier, and that's where I intend to go," he said.

That same month, the National Aeronautics and Space Administration (NASA) announced it would choose a new group of astronauts. Both Neil and Mike applied. So did Buzz Aldrin. (A few women applied too, but NASA wanted only male astronauts.)

Buzz was in New England going to the Massachusetts Institute of Technology (MIT). He was studying ways that astronauts could guide spacecraft to come together, or dock, in orbit. When he wrote about this topic, Buzz dedicated his paper to members of the space program. "If only I could join them in their exciting endeavors!" he wrote.

Jerrie Cobb (RIGHT) was the first woman to pass the tests to become an astronaut. But NASA did not send a woman into space until 1983.

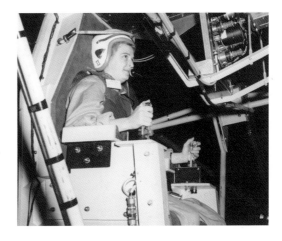

More than 250 other candidates applied to NASA to become astronauts. Neil was one of the nine pilots chosen. Buzz and Mike were not. But they tried again when NASA called for more applications the next year.

Their determination paid off. On October 17, 1963, NASA announced the names of fourteen new astronauts. Mike and Buzz were among them. They were eager to begin their training.

Buzz (FRONT ROW, FAR LEFT) and Mike (BACK ROW, FAR LEFT) were chosen to become NASA astronauts.

NATIONAL GOAL

During the 1950s and 1960s, the United States and the Soviet Union did not trust each other. The Soviet Union was a large nation made up of Russia and fourteen nearby countries. Both the United States and the Soviet Union wanted to be number one in military strength and in space exploration. The Soviets launched the first satellite, *Sputnik*, in 1957. Three and a half years later, they sent the first man, Yury Gagarin, into Earth orbit. But President John Kennedy thought the United States could still win the space race. In May 1961, he announced, "I believe this nation should commit itself, before this decade is out, to landing a man on the moon and returning him safely to the earth."

3 ORBITING EARTH

The United States wanted to beat the Soviet Union in the space race. While the world watched, NASA launched one space mission after another. Neil was chosen as command pilot for the two-person Gemini 8 mission. The flight took off on March 16, 1966.

David Scott (LEFT) and Neil (RIGHT) in the GEMINI 8 spacecraft

Neil and his crewmate, David Scott, successfully docked with an unmanned vehicle—a spacecraft with no one aboard. Then something went wrong. The spacecraft began to tumble wildly. The motion was making Neil sick. He couldn't see clearly. He feared that both he and David might pass out. Thinking quickly, Neil started up another control system. His plan worked. The spinning stopped. But the two astronauts had to return to Earth.

NASA chose John W. Young (LEFT) and Mike (RIGHT) for the Gemini 10 mission.

Four months later, in July, Mike got his turn in space aboard *Gemini 10*. During the flight, Mike made two space walks. In the first, he stood on his seat and reached outside the spacecraft. Mike did some experiments and took some pictures. Later, he left the spacecraft completely. Protected by his space suit, Mike was joined to the spacecraft by a life-support line.

Buzz spends time outside of his spacecraft during the Gemini 12 mission.

Buzz had a chance to walk in space too. On November 11, 1966, he set off on the four-day Gemini 12 mission. He spent almost two hours outside the spacecraft. This set a new record.

During the Gemini program, astronauts gained important skills and knowledge. They stayed in space for up to two weeks. They learned how to handle themselves in the weightlessness of space. And, like Mike and Buzz, they mastered leaving the craft to walk and work in space. By the end of 1966, the Gemini program gave way to the Apollo program. The goal of the Apollo program was to put a man on the moon.

Rockets launch the
APOLLO 8 spacecraft
into space.

Neil Armstrong awoke
at three in the morning on
December 21, 1968. *Apollo 8* was scheduled
to launch that day. NASA officials were
especially excited. For the first time, men
would try to orbit the moon. Neil was
backup commander for the flight. Although
he wouldn't be going into space, he went
through the same training as the astronauts
who would. Neil watched the mission blast
off early in the morning.

The next day, Deke Slayton, the head of the astronaut office, told Neil that he had been chosen to lead the Apollo 11 mission. Its goal depended on the success of the Apollo 8, 9, and 10 missions. Neil was happy when *Apollo 8* circled the moon.

On January 4, 1969, Deke told Mike and Buzz that they had been assigned to the crew of *Apollo 11*. "[It] . . . may work out that this will be the first lunar [moon] landing attempt," Deke said.

CREWMATES

Neil, Buzz, and Mike had very different personalities. Mike was talkative and imaginative. Neil tended to be quiet. Buzz had lots of ideas. He was deeply focused on his work. The *Apollo 11* crew members never became close friends, but they respected and liked one another. One time, Neil joked, "As an old navy guy, I think I did remarkably well in getting along with two air force guys."

4 "THE EAGLE HAS LANDED"

The astronauts lived and trained in Houston, Texas. But space missions took off from Cape Canaveral in Florida. On July 16, 1969, officials and reporters from all over the world came to see the launch of *Apollo 11*. Half a million people jammed the area surrounding the cape. Neil felt certain that the crew would return to Earth safely. But would they really be able to land on the moon? He thought their chances were only about fifty-fifty.

The APOLLO 11 spacecraft begins its trip into space.

"We have liftoff!" announced NASA at 9:32 A.M. A three-thousand-ton rocket lifted *Apollo 11* into space. The men's pulses were racing. They were about to attempt something no one had ever done.

Four days later, the astronauts were circling the moon. By that time, the spacecraft had split into two parts, or modules. Mike stayed in lunar orbit in the command module, named *Columbia*. Neil and Buzz prepared to travel the final sixty-nine miles to the moon. They rode in a specially designed lunar module called the *Eagle*.

As they got close to the moon, several alarms went off. NASA officials decided that the computer was overloaded. But the astronauts were not in danger. "You are Go [safe] to land," mission control told them.

The *Eagle* was only one thousand feet above the moon. Looking out, Neil saw a crater, or hole, as big as a football field. Boulders surrounded the crater. It was not a safe place to land. The computer had been controlling the *Eagle*. Taking over, Neil steered the craft in search of a better landing site.

The *Eagle* was using up its fuel quickly. If the astronauts did not land soon, they would have to cancel their mission. Then Neil saw a large, flat area. He had less than a minute to spare. Neil headed the *Eagle* toward the new landing site.

The Columbia took this picture of the moon's surface. The big crater in the middle is 50 miles (80 kilometers) wide.

Rockets helped the *Eagle* slow down. The force of the rockets churned up great clouds of dust. The craft touched down softly. The astronauts could hardly tell when they stopped. "The *Eagle* has landed," Neil radioed. His words thrilled people all over the world.

Several hours later, Neil stood in his space suit on the ladder outside the lunar module. "One small step for man," he said. Then he made the three-foot jump from the bottom of the ladder to the moon. "One giant leap for mankind." A television camera sent his voice and image to 600 million people on Earth.

Neil took this picture of Buzz stepping off the ladder.

MOON GRAVITY

Walking on the moon is not the same as walking on Earth. In their space suits with the heavy backpacks, each astronaut weighed about 360 pounds on Earth. But the moon's gravity is much less than Earth's. Less gravity means you weigh less. On the moon, the astronauts weighed only 60 pounds each. Part of Buzz's job was to try out different ways of moving around in the low gravity. He had fun testing such walks as the "skipping stride" and the "kangaroo hop."

The surface of the moon was covered with fine, dark particles. Some people had feared walking on the moon would be hard. But Neil found it easy. "It has a stark beauty all its own," said Neil. "It's very pretty out here."

Meanwhile, Buzz could hardly wait to reach the surface too. "Beautiful view!" he declared when he exited the spacecraft. The moon might be barren and lifeless. But it looked "magnificent" to Buzz.

Neil (LEFT) and Buzz (RIGHT) brought a U.S. flag to leave on the moon.

The two men set to work at once. They set up a U.S. flag. They uncovered a plaque on one of the *Eagle's* landing legs. Neil read the words on the plaque for all the people watching on Earth. "Here men from the Planet Earth first set foot upon the Moon, July 1969 A.D. We came in peace for all mankind."

The astronauts gathered rocks and soil to take back to Earth. They set up experiments. One would measure moonquakes. Another would help scientists measure the exact distance between Earth and the moon. Neil and Buzz also took lots of photos. Even a simple picture of a footprint in the lunar soil became famous around the world.

Buzz walks near a leg of the lunar module. This picture shows the footprints in the soil around him.

5 "NOT CHAINED TO THIS PLANET"

All too soon, the two hours and forty minutes allowed for the moonwalk were over. The men would have liked to stay longer. But their life-support systems would last only a short time.

Neil and Buzz spent an uncomfortable night in the cramped lunar module. Then it was time to go home. The countdown to liftoff was a tense moment. If something went wrong, Neil and Buzz would be stranded. The command module had no landing gear. Mike would not be able to land to rescue them.

To everyone's relief, the launch went perfectly. The *Eagle* rose to lunar orbit and docked with the *Columbia*. A very relieved Mike Collins welcomed his crewmates back.

The EAGLE rises above the moon's surface. This picture was taken from the COLUMBIA before the EAGLE docked.

Neil, Buzz, and Mike never forgot the sight of Earth as they headed home. "It is wonderful to look out the window and see [the moon] shrinking and the tiny Earth growing," Mike said later. On July 24, the spacecraft splashed down in the Pacific Ocean.

The astronauts wait in a raft after their spacecraft lands.

President Nixon visits the astronauts in quarantine.

A naval helicopter picked up the astronauts. It took them to the aircraft carrier *Hornet*. Crowds cheered as the helicopter landed on deck. President Nixon was also there to greet the astronauts. Neil, Buzz, and Mike immediately went into quarantine. This meant they were kept apart from everyone else. Doctors wanted to make sure they were not carrying any moon germs that might spread to others.

Everyone wanted to see the astronauts after they came out of quarantine. Swarms of people turned out for a parade to honor them in New York City. The air was thick with confetti.

Neil, Buzz, and Mike were invited
to speak to the U.S. Congress. There,
they received a hero's welcome. In late
September, they set off with their wives on
a worldwide trip called Giant Step. Many
world leaders welcomed them. They even
met with the shah of Iran and the emperor of
Japan. Between 100 million and 150 million
people cheered the astronauts and listened
to their message of goodwill. "More can be
gained from friendship than from technical
knowledge," Neil said later that year.

Buzz, Mike, and Neil wave to a parade crowd in Spain.

NASA designed this symbol for the Apollo 11 mission. It shows a bald eagle landing on the moon.

None of the astronauts flew a mission into space again. But they helped the space program in other important ways. For several years, Neil taught at the University of Cincinnati. In 1986, he served on the committee to look into the tragic explosion of the space shuttle *Challenger*. And he continues to fly airplanes.

After retiring from the air force, Buzz wrote books. He took part in film projects that promote space exploration. He also opened a company to promote tourism in space. He believes that one day tourists will orbit Earth. Meanwhile, he has designed a permanent space station. In 2001, President George W. Bush named Buzz to the Commission on the Future of the United States Aerospace Industry.

Almost two years after the *Apollo 11* flight, Mike became the first director of the National Air and Space Museum. That is one of the popular Smithsonian museums in Washington, D.C. In 1978, he moved up to become an undersecretary of the Smithsonian Institution. When he left, he became vice president of an aerospace company in Virginia. Five years later, he started a business to give advice about flying.

WHERE DID THE MOON COME FROM?

The six Apollo missions helped scientists learn more about the moon. They developed a new idea of how the moon was formed. Many scientists believe a large planet hit Earth long ago. The collision knocked off a great deal of rocks and dust. Over a long period of time, this matter came together as the moon.

Mike (LEFT), Neil (MIDDLE), and Buzz (RIGHT) in 1999

As of 2009, six Apollo missions have landed on the moon. The last one was in 1972. The United States went on to develop the Skylab and space shuttle programs. Astronauts lived and worked in space, but they did not go to the moon or any other planets.

Soon that may change. NASA has announced plans for future lunar missions. Neil, Buzz, and Mike welcome the idea. As Neil said in 1999, the Apollo program had showed "that humanity is not forever chained to this planet . . . and our opportunities are unlimited."

TIMELINE

BUZZ ALDRIN WAS BORN ON
JANUARY 20, 1930
NEIL ARMSTRONG WAS BORN ON
AUGUST 5, 1930
MIKE COLLINS WAS BORN ON
OCTOBER 31, 1930

In the year . . .

1949   Neil was called from college to serve in the navy.   Age 19

1951   Neil's plane was shot down in Korea.

Buzz graduated from West Point.

1952   Buzz was sent to Korea as a fighter pilot.   Age 22

Mike graduated from West Point.

1955   Neil graduated from Purdue University.

Neil became a test pilot at Edwards Air Force Base.

1962   Neil was chosen as an astronaut.   Age 32

1963   Buzz received a doctorate from MIT.

Mike and Buzz were chosen as astronauts.

1966   Neil commanded the Gemini 8 mission.

Mike flew on the Gemini 10 mission.

Buzz flew on the Gemini 12 mission.

1968   The *Apollo 8* astronauts became the first men to orbit the moon.

1969   Neil and Buzz became the first men to walk on the moon on July 20.

Neil, Buzz, and Mike began a world tour.

1971   Neil became a professor at the University of Cincinnati.

Mike became the director of the National Air and Space Museum.

1986   Neil helped to investigate the disaster of the space shuttle *Challenger.*

2001   Buzz was named to the Commission on the Future of the United States Aerospace Industry.

THE LUNAR MODULE

The lunar module had a big job to do. It had to carry twelve tons of fuel. It had to land on an alien land. And it had to keep the astronauts alive.

Engineers worked more than six years to design a spacecraft that could meet these demands. Led by a man named Tom Kelly, three thousand people worked on the lunar module. To save weight, the module had no seats. The astronauts had to fly standing up. They were not allowed to bring toothbrushes or soap with them. Even that small additional weight was considered too much. The lunar module was so lightweight that some people called it the "tissue paper spacecraft."

The landing stage of the *Apollo 11*'s lunar module, the *Eagle*, was left behind. When Neil and Buzz returned to the command ship, they had to set the rest of the *Eagle* free. It was hard to say good-bye to the craft that had protected them. But its weight would make the return home harder.

For several years, the *Eagle* remained in orbit. Eventually it crashed onto the moon's surface. But visitors to the Air and Space Museum in Washington, D.C., can see a lunar module (*right*) like the one that took Neil and Buzz to the moon.

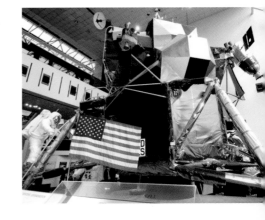

FURTHER READING

Aldrin, Buzz. *Look to the Stars*. New York: Penguin Group, 2009. The second man on the moon talks about humankind's search for the stars, beginning with astronomers Copernicus and Galileo.

Aldrin, Buzz. *Reaching for the Moon*. New York: HarperCollins, 2005. In this picture book, Buzz Aldrin describes his childhood and experiences as an astronaut.

Platt, Richard. *Moon Landing: A Pop-Up Celebration of Apollo 11*. Somerville, MA: Candlewick Press, 2008. This pop-up book lets you see the lunar module, the moon, and a rocket.

Schyffert, Bea Uusma. *The Man Who Went to the Far Side of the Moon: The Story of* Apollo 11 *Astronaut Michael Collins*. San Francisco: Chronicle Books, 2003. Schyffert's biography tells the story of the Apollo 11 achievement.

Zemlicka, Shannon. *Neil Armstrong*. Minneapolis: Lerner Publications Company, 2002. Zemlicka's lively biography describes Neil's life and the Apollo 11 mission.

WEBSITES

Project Apollo: Astronaut Biographies
http://www.hq.nasa.gov/office/pao/History/ap11ann/astrobios.htm This site has biographies of Buzz Aldrin, Neil Armstrong, and Michael Collins as well as shorter biographies of other *Apollo* astronauts.

The Space Place: Home
http://spaceplace.nasa.gov/en/kids/ This NASA site has a variety of activities, including one that lets you build a

moon habitat. Help prepare the astronauts to return to the moon.

StarChild: Apollo 11
http://starchild.gsfc.nasa.gov/docs/StarChild/space_level2/apollo11.html This site gives a brief description of the Apollo 11 mission and offers links to movies about the landing and the "first steps on the moon."

SELECT BIBLIOGRAPHY

Armstrong, Neil, Stephen E. Ambrose, and Douglas Brinkley. "NASA Johnson Space Center Oral History Project: Oral History Transcript: Neil Armstrong." *NASA History*, September 19, 2001. http://www.history.nasa.gov/alsj/a11/ArmstrongNA_9-19-01.pdf (March 18, 2009).

Chaikin, Andrew. *A Man on the Moon: The Voyages of the Apollo Astronauts.* New York: Penguin Books, 1994.

Hansen, James. *First Man: The Life of Neil A. Armstrong.* New York: Simon & Schuster Paperbacks, 2005.

NASA. "*Apollo 11* 30th Anniversary Press Conference." July 16, 1999. *Nasa History.* September 20, 2002. http://history.nasa.gov/ap11ann/pressconf.htm (November 30, 2008).

Pyle, Ron. *Destination Moon: The Apollo Missions in the Astronauts' Own Words.* New York: First Person Productions Collins, 2005.

Reynolds, David West. *Apollo: The Epic Journey to the Moon.* New York: Tehabi Book, 2002.

INDEX

Acknowledgments

For photographs and artwork: The images in this book are used with the permission of: © MPI/Hulton Archive/Getty Images, p. 4; Ohio Historical Society, pp. 7, 8; Courtesy of Dr. Buzz Aldrin, pp. 9, 10; AP Photo, pp. 11, 15; © Russell Lee/Library of Congress/Hulton Archive/Getty Images, p. 12; NASA/DFRC, pp. 14, 16, 18; NASA/KSC, pp. 17, 29, 30; NASA/GRC, p. 19; NASA/JSC, pp. 20, 25, 31, 32, 34, 35, 37, 39, 41; AP Photo/NASA, pp. 23, 26; © NASA/Time & Life Pictures/Getty Images, pp. 24, 38; © Paul Popper/Popperfoto/Getty Images, p. 40; AP Photo/Doug Mills, p. 43; © Alex Segre/Alamy, p. 45. Front Cover: © NASA/ Time & Life Pictures/Getty Images. Back Cover: NASA/JSC.

For quoted material: For quoted material: pp. 7, 19, 27 (both), 32, 33, 34, 38, 40, James Hansen, *The Life of Neil A. Armstrong* (New York: Simon & Schuster, 2005); pp. 18, 26, 30, 33, Andrew Chaikin, *A Man on the Moon: The Voyages of the Apollo Astronauts* (New York: Penguin Books, 1994); pp. 29, 32, David West Reynolds, *Apollo: The Epic Journey to the Moon* (New York: Tehabi Books, 2002); pp. 33, 45, Ron Pyle, *Destination Moon: The Apollo Missions in the Astronauts' Own Words,* (New York: First Person Productions Collins, 2005); p. 43, *Apollo 11 30th Anniversary* Press Conference, Kennedy Space Center, July 16, 1999. http:// history.nasa.gov/apllann/pressconf.htm.